THE FLIPPED I

T0273193

flipped learning

for
Math
INSTRUCTION

JONATHAN BERGMANN
AARON SAMS

International Society for Technology in Education
EUGENE, OREGON • ARLINGTON, VIRGINIA

The Flipped Learning Series
Flipped Learning for Math Instruction
Jonathan Bergmann and Aaron Sams

Editor: *Paul Wurster*
Associate Editor: *Emily Reed*
Production Manager: *Lynda Gansel*
Copy Editor: *Kristin Landon*
Proofreader: *Ann Skaugset*
Cover Design: *Brianne Beigh*
Book Design and Production: *Kim McGovern*

First Edition
ISBN: 978-1-56484-360-9 (paperback)
ISBN: 978-1-56484-501-6 (e-book)

Printed in the United States of America

About ISTE

The International Society for Technology in Education (ISTE) is the premier nonprofit organization serving educators and education leaders committed to empowering connected learners in a connected world. ISTE serves more than 100,000 education stakeholders throughout the world.

ISTE's innovative offerings include the ISTE Conference & Expo, one of the biggest, most comprehensive ed tech events in the world—as well as the widely adopted ISTE Standards for learning, teaching and leading in the digital age and a robust suite of professional learning resources, including webinars, online courses, consulting services for schools and districts, books, and peer-reviewed journals and publications. Visit iste.org to learn more.

Also by Jonathan Bergmann and Aaron Sams

Flipped Learning: Gateway to Student Engagement

Flip Your Classroom: Reach Every Student in Every Class Every Day

Flip Your Classroom—The Workbook: Making Flipped Learning Work for You

About the Authors

Jon Bergmann is a teacher who used to love being the center of the classroom. But he gave it up when he saw how engaged his students became in the learning process when he began flipping his instruction. Flipped learning allowed him to know his students better, which brought him back to the reason he became a teacher in the first place. He is considered one of the pioneers of flipped learning and now shares his passion for learner-centered classrooms with educators around the globe. Jon is currently chief learning officer of FlippedClass.com. He received the Presidential Award for Excellence in Math and Science Teaching in 2002 and was named a semifinalist for Colorado Teacher of the Year in 2010. Jon serves on the advisory board of TED Education and hosts "The Flip Side," a radio show that tells the stories of flipped educators. In addition, he is a founding board member and the treasurer of the Flipped Learning Network, the only not-for-profit organization run by and for flipped educators.

Aaron Sams has been an educator since 2000. He is managing director of FlippedClass.com, is co-founder of The Flipped Learning Network, and is an adjunct professor at Saint Vincent College. He was awarded the 2009 Presidential Award for Excellence in Math and Science Teaching and was a chemistry teacher in Woodland Park, CO, and in Hacienda Heights, CA. Aaron also served as co-chair of the Colorado State Science Standards Revision Committee and serves as an advisor to TED-Ed. Aaron co-authored *Flip Your Classroom: Reach Every Student in Every Class Every Day* and *Flipped Learning: Gateway to Student Engagement.* He frequently speaks and conducts workshops on educational uses of screencasts and the flipped classroom concept. He advocates for inquiry-based and student-centered learning environments in which students are encouraged to demonstrate their understanding in ways that are meaningful to them. With experience in public, private, and home schools, in face-to-face, online, and blended learning environments, Aaron brings a unique educational perspective to any audience. He is a lifelong learner, reader, maker, and explorer. He holds a BS in Biochemistry and an MAEd, both from Biola University.

Contents

Preface

As the first days of school began in 2006, we—Aaron Sams and Jonathan Bergmann—arrived to teach science at Woodland Park High School in Woodland Park, Colorado. Jon came from the Denver metropolitan area and settled into room 313, and Aaron came from the greater Los Angeles area to occupy room 314.

We had both taught chemistry at our previous schools, Jon for 18 years and Aaron for 6 years. Because we represented the entire chemistry team, we decided to work together to develop a strong chemistry program at Woodland Park.

During the school year, we taught traditionally, using a great deal of direct instruction in an engaging lecture style. We also met on a regular basis to reflect about best practices and how to integrate technology into our classes. These voluntary meetings grew out of the fact that we worked together well and realized that two heads were better than one.

In the spring of 2007, Aaron showed Jon an article that reviewed a computer program that recorded PowerPoint lectures, including digital ink that could be written on the screen and audio recording. At this point, we were ready to dive into the world of teacher-created video.

We first used screen-recording software to capture live lectures. Once we started, the assistant superintendent in charge of curriculum and instruction in our school district took note and visited our classrooms. Her daughter was attending a university, and one of her daughter's professors was recording the audio of his lectures. She told us that her daughter loved this model because she didn't have to go to class anymore. Later that week during lunch, a conversation about that interaction ensued. What is the value of class time if a student can access all the content while not attending class? Why do students really need a teacher physically present?

In that conversation Aaron asked Jon, "What if we stopped lecturing in class and pre-recorded all of our lessons, and in class students could do the stuff that they used to do at home?" Jon said, "OK, let's do it!" Since then, neither of us has used direct instruction as a whole-group, in-class teaching method.

During this time of development, we shared online with a group of teachers what we were doing. These teachers had been active on the AP Chemistry listserv for many years, and they used that platform to connect and learn from other AP Chemistry teachers from around the world. As the concept of the flipped classroom grew, this group became a place to share and learn, serving as a sounding board as well. So the flipped classroom was not born in a vacuum. It did not develop in rooms 313 and 314 alone.

There are now many communities of practice around the world for teachers who are implementing the flipped class. We, along with Dr. Jerry Overmeyer at the University of Northern Colorado, oversee one community at flippedclassroom.org that has more than 25,000 members. Though we get much of the credit for the flipped classroom, it would never have happened without the broader network of other amazing teachers.

The idea of the flipped classroom is really quite simple. Direct instruction is done through video, or some other digital learning object, which students can individually use before they come to class. This time shift allows the teacher to use class time for work that is either better done as a large group or requires individualized attention by the teacher. That's it! The flipped class, in brief, is direct instruction delivered to the individual outside of class so there is more strategic use of in-class time for group work and individualized attention. We soon found out that we had stumbled onto something that could radically transform our classrooms into something we never could have anticipated.

We have chronicled much of this in our previous books, *Flip Your Classroom: Reach Every Student in Every Class Every Day* (Bergmann & Sams, 2012) and *Flipped Learning: Gateway to Student Engagement* (Bergmann & Sams, 2014). Since the publication of those two books, teachers have been asking us for very specific resources on how to flip different subjects and grade levels. This book is part of a series of books designed to meet that demand.

This book is a practical guide for mathematics teachers interested in flipping their classrooms. It helps real math teachers deal with the realities of teaching in an increasingly interconnected and digital world. This book serves as a guide for math teachers who are beginning to flip their classes, or are interested in exploring the flipped model for the first time. Each chapter explores practical ways to bring flipped learning into the math classroom, including:

- How to flip your class, and the four hurdles to flipping (thinking, technology, time, and training).

- How your approach to planning changes as you implement flipped learning.

- How flipping will enhance the practical mathematics experience for students.

- How you can use traditional resources such as textbooks and the internet.

- What to do in class once you have flipped your class.

- How to implement the flipped-mastery model into a math classroom.

- How flipped learning can work alongside learning through inquiry.

- How flipped learning can provide an environment where projects can be done more often and with more fidelity.

We begin with a story about a teacher who flipped his class—and found it transformed.

Chapter 1

why you should flip your class

FLIPPED LEARNING has a deep impact on the professional lives of teachers, but more important, flipped learning positively affects the lives of students. Adam Johnson teaches eighth grade math in Alabama. Adam believes that at every level, whether you are teaching fourth grade math or college calculus, students are novices. For them, every new lesson is their first exposure to a particular math concept. Teachers need to assume there is some subject matter students don't know and should find ways to bring each student to a greater level of understanding.

Half of Adam's students have Individual Education Plans (IEPs) or 504s, and the other half are placed in his classes because they struggle with math. Many of his students enter his class lagging behind in math skills. They need extra time and practice, and teaching them is a challenging task. Adam was struggling to meet the individual needs of these students. He was seeking a way to provide them with the help they needed and to make math engaging for his students. Adam wanted his students to be good at math and to *feel* that they were good at math. He wanted them to gain the confidence and skills they needed to become successful in a world where mathematics played such a critical role.

Three years ago, Adam discovered the flipped classroom model and began to flip his class using videos he found online. He had some success, but he felt underwhelmed with the flipped classroom. In the fall of 2013, he attended a workshop led by Jon and discovered some key elements that helped him take his flipped class to the next level. Many of the things Adam learned in that one-day workshop helped him implement the model with efficacy and fidelity. His students are now excited about math. They are discussing math with each other and have grown increasingly confident in their skills.

Adam cites a few reasons why math teachers should consider the Flipped Classroom model:

- The flipped classroom model has *engaged* his students in mathematics. They are no longer passive recipients of information.

- The key to making the flipped classroom work is to capitalize on opportunities for *individualization*, which this model affords.

- He has developed a *culture of learning,* leading to students who are more successful.

- The flipped classroom model gives him the *time* to help his struggling students. He simply has more one-on-one and small-group interactions with his students.

- A teacher should foster a *healthy level of frustration* in the classroom. Students need cognitive dissonance, with support, to grow in their mathematical understanding.

- The flipped classroom *lowers the walls of the schoolhouse.* School is transparent to the parents, helping them understand what their children are learning and empowering them to assist as their children practice and learn.

Enoch Ng, a Grade 5–6 math teacher in Singapore, teaches in what is known as a "low profile" school. In the past, many of his students did not perform well in school, especially in math. As Enoch watched his students struggle, he felt as though he was hitting a wall. He was frustrated that he was unable to help his struggling students or his advanced ones. The only students he felt he was reaching were a few in the middle. That is when he stumbled onto a few online videos about flipped learning and became intrigued. Because he had previously tried (and failed) to engage his students using technology, he was skeptical. Despite this reservation, he knew what he was doing wasn't working, and that he owed it to his students to do whatever it took to engage them and help them understand math. As he began to implement flipped learning, he realized that there was a way to help the vast majority of his students. Now, more of his students are understanding, learning, and enjoying math. They are now engaged in projects and understand how mathematics apply to real life. Enoch is now able to meet the needs of all his students. With his typical 40 students per class, classroom management used to be very difficult. Since Enoch started flipping his classroom, management struggles have virtually disappeared.

Enoch went on to share his journey with his colleagues, and this initially encouraged three other math teachers to flip. With the program's success, three more teachers have joined the group. They plan flipped videos in their weekly meetings, but more important, the teachers have rich conversations about math, pedagogy, and how to best meet their students' needs. Flipped learning has transformed Enoch's class into a center of learning, and it has done the same to his colleagues' classrooms.

Flipped Class 101

Simplicity is the ultimate sophistication.
—LEONARDO DA VINCI

Sometimes the simplest ideas are the most profound. Think back to BlackBerry phones, with their many buttons. Everybody wanted one until Steve Jobs, of Apple, told his design team to create a phone with *one* button. As they say, the rest is history. The flipped class technique is a simple idea at its core, based on these two steps:

- Move the direct instruction (often called the lecture) away from the group space. This usually means that students watch and interact with an instructional video (flipped video) prior to coming to class.

- Repurpose class time that you freed up from direct instruction and use it to practice learned concepts, engaging activities, and higher-order thinking.

We call this simple time-shift Flipped Class 101, which reflects what people popularly refer to as a flipped classroom. Flip the homework with the direct instruction, and you have a flipped class. This simple time-shift has significant benefits, such as the following:

- In a typical classroom, students often go home with difficult homework. They do this work independently and have little or no help. Some are successful, but many are not. In a flipped class, students do the difficult tasks in class in the presence of an expert, the teacher.

- Because the presentation of content is removed from class time, there is more time for teachers to interact and help students.

- Students can pause and rewind a video. In a typical class, you cannot pause your teacher.

There are many other benefits, which we have chronicled in our aforementioned previous books. Recognizing those benefits, the focus of this book is to give math teachers practical strategies to help them reach students using the flipped model.

The One Question

Another way to think about the simplicity of the flipped classroom model is to boil it down to one simple question: *What is the best use of your face-to-face class time?* Is this valuable time with students best spent on content dissemination of information, or should it be used for something else? In a flipped classroom setting, the direct instruction is offloaded to the individual space, and the class time is used for something else. In math classes, this "something else" is more hands-on activities, more inquiry, more projects, and more guided practice time with the teacher.

When we flipped our classes, our students performed significantly better on our unit exams, enabling us to do 50% more hands-on activities (Bergmann & Sams, 2012). What started as an experiment to help meet the needs of our students became a new technique that radically changed our classrooms and the classrooms of many other teachers.

Given that we experienced success with this model, you would expect that we would continue to use it. However, after the first year of the flipped class we didn't simply repeat the previous year—we reinvented our class again, adding mastery learning to our repertoire. Based on the work of Benjamin Bloom (1968), the flipped-mastery model is an asynchronous approach in which students demonstrate mastery of content before moving on to new topics. Each student moves at a flexible pace, which allows advanced students to get the challenges they need and provides extra support for struggling students.

Beyond the Flipped Class

Why do we call it Flipped Class 101? Though we believe the flipped class is a viable method, with benefits over more traditional forms of instruction, we believe you can take the flipped class to the next level. We see teachers flip their classrooms for 1 or 2 years and then move to deeper learning strategies, such as flipped-mastery, or a more inquiry- or project-based model. We do not categorize these as a flipped classroom, but as flipped learning. Flipped learning is the second iteration of the flipped classroom, where teachers move *beyond* the basic Flipped Class 101 model to more content-rich, inquiry-driven, and project-based classes. We chronicle this transformation well in our book *Flipped Learning: Gateway to Student Engagement.* We will share how these strategies work, specifically in a math class, toward the end of this book. For now, let's explore Flipped Class 101 a little more deeply.

Chapter 2

flipped class
101

THOUGH THE FLIPPED CLASSROOM model is a simple idea, it can be complex for teachers to implement. Simply telling students to watch a video and then come to class to learn more deeply sounds good, but what if students don't watch the video? What if students don't have access to technology at home? What is a teacher to do then?

There are four major hurdles to flipping that you need to overcome. These are:

- Flipping your thinking

- Technological barriers

- Finding the time

- Training yourself, students, and parents

Flipping Your Thinking

Flipping your thinking as a math teacher may be the *most* important hurdle to overcome. Why is this a big hurdle? Perhaps it is because many of us have been "doing school" the same way for many years and find change to be difficult.

Jon spent 19 years as a lecture/discussion teacher. He knew very well how to teach that way. In fact, he reached the point where if you told him the topic of the day, he could probably start teaching that topic without any notes, simply from his years of experience. In 2007, when we decided to begin using video as our primary means of direct instruction, Jon was the hesitant one. He didn't want to give up lecture time. He was a good lecturer (or at least he thought he was). He liked being the center of attention and enjoyed engaging a whole group of students in science instruction. His class was well structured, and he liked being in control of all that was happening. So, when he flipped his class, he had to surrender control of the learning to the students. That was not easy, but it was the best thing he ever did in his teaching career.

Anyone born before the 1990s grew up in an information-scarce world. We had to search through card catalogs and microfiche to access information. Information was localized at the schoolhouses, in textbooks and libraries, and in the heads of our teachers. Today, students can access virtually any information by simply accessing a device they most likely have in their pocket.

In light of this change, we must rethink how we teach our students. Think of any topic you currently teach— for example, adding fractions, the quadratic formula, or solving a differential equation. A quick search of YouTube reveals a myriad of videos available to explain these concepts. So the bigger question is this: How do we teach when our students have an oversupply of information?

Technological Barriers of the Flipped Classroom

Many educators have pigeonholed the flipped class model as a technological solution to education. Much of the buzz about flipping has to do with using video as an instructional tool, which does involve a technological component. However, we disagree with those who see flipped learning as a technology-based educational practice. We see flipped learning as a pedagogical solution with an underlying technological component.

What, then, are the technological tools you need to master to flip your math class?

Teachers often ask us, "What is the best tool to flip my class?" To this question we respond, "It is the one you will *actually* use." Our answer has a lot to do with you and your skills and needs. What type of a computer do you have? Do you have tablets? Do your students have devices? What is your comfort level with technology?

There is a whole host of available technological tools. Some are very easy to use and are limited in features, whereas others are more complicated, offering more powerful features that add to the production values of your content. We understand that not all teachers are tech experts, so the tool you might use has a high degree of variability. We do see a few categories of technological tools that teachers must master to flip a class effectively. Before we discuss them, we should address a key question.

Who Should Make the Videos?

Should you make the flipped videos when there are already videos on every conceivable math topic on YouTube? There is no question that anything you teach has probably been posted, but we believe that one of the hallmarks of a successful flipped classroom is the use of videos created by the teacher or a team of teachers at the local school. When we visit *struggling* flipped classrooms, we often see that the teacher is simply assigning video content created either commercially or by teachers outside their immediate network rather than making their own. Conversely, when we walk into *successful* flipped classrooms, we usually find that the teacher is the video creator. We think the reason teacher-created videos are more successful is because they involve one of the fundamental features of good teaching: relationships with kids who know you! You are their teacher. Some random person on the internet is *not* as familiar. Students see your investment in them through the content you provide. They recognize that someone who has direct involvement in their lives created custom content for them.

Video Creation Tools

As of the writing of this book (bearing in mind that technology tools are always in flux), we continually observe five categories of video creation tools teachers are using to create flipped class videos: cameras, document cameras, screencasting programs, tablet apps, and smart pens.

Video cameras. The easiest tool for most teachers to use is the camera built into their phone. Virtually all modern mobile phones have a video camera built in. Also, inexpensive handheld video cameras are capable of producing very high-quality video. A teacher could have someone (a colleague or student) use a camera or phone to record them teaching a concept at a chalkboard. This is ideal for demonstrating how to solve a second order polynomial or virtually any sort of algorithmic math. This method would not be as good for topics where you would need extensive pictures, such as discussing geometric shapes.

Document cameras. Many teachers have used their document cameras to make flipped class videos. Many don't realize that this camera, which is designed to project an image in real time, can also record. When the document camera is hooked up to a computer (typically through a USB port), the software that came with the document camera often has the ability to record the screen. Therefore, the work a teacher performs under the document camera can be recorded, along with the teacher's voice. For example, this method would work well if you would like to demonstrate how to find the area of a circle and you want students to see your work. A more powerful use of this technique might be using manipulatives to demonstrate fractions or place value. You can then convert all of this into a video and share it with students.

Screencasting programs. These programs record whatever is happening on your computer screen along with audio, and in some cases, even a webcam shot. Screencasting is the number-one choice for flipped class teachers to make videos. Typically, they create a lesson or presentation in some sort of presentation software, such as Microsoft PowerPoint, and use a screencasting program to record them teaching through their slide deck. There are even ways for the teacher to digitally write on the presentation so the students view the presentation, hear the teacher's voice, see a webcam of the teacher in the corner, and see whatever the teacher writes on the screen.

Tablet apps. Many apps for tablet devices can be used to make video recordings. Some popular apps include:

- Knowmia (www.knowmia.com)

- Explain Everything (www.morriscooke.com)

- Doceri (http://doceri.com)

- Educreations (www.educreations.com)

One advantage of tablet devices is that it is easy to write on the presentation. For many of these apps you can upload a presentation to the tablet and then record the presentation. The tablet interface is an ideal choice when you need to annotate over pictures or want to have typical chalkboard features.

Smart pens. There are a variety of smart pens available that will digitally record what you write on paper as well as record your voice. These recordings are then converted into video files (often called pencasts) and can be shared on the internet. Some of these pens require special paper that you can purchase or print online.

Hosting Videos

Once you finish creating a video, you must upload it to the internet for students to access. A large number of video hosting sites are available. The easiest and most familiar to use is YouTube, assuming your school district does not block that site. YouTube is good in that the vast majority of students know how to access it, and their handheld devices most certainly play those videos.

But if you don't want to or cannot post YouTube videos, there are other video hosting sites available, like Vimeo, TeacherTube, or Screencast.com. You can also post videos to the school website or to a learning management system (LMS).

Making Videos Interactive

Once you have created a flipped video and posted it online, it is important to have students do more than simply watch the video. Video watching is a passive activity. Students are familiar with viewing Hollywood movies, where they sit and watch something designed to entertain them. Watching an instructional video, where students must come away with some level of under-standing, is a very different activity. We recommend that teachers build interactivity into the videos. There is no single way to do this. You could have students simply take notes on the video, have them respond to an online forum, or use some other creative strategy. There are even software and web tools available that pause video at specified times, causing a teacher-generated question to pop up. The teacher then has access to user logs to identify who watched their video, and how each student responded to its questions. Regardless of which tool is used, the key is to make sure that students are actively engaged with the content and have something to do as they watch.

Making Flipped Videos Easy to Access

It is important to find an easy way to post video content, but it is equally (and maybe more) important to make it easy for students to access the videos. Learning management systems (LMS) are a category of websites that allow a teacher or entire school to organize digital content in one place. Students log in and interact with digital content in some way. An LMS can host videos, store online documents for students to view, and have forums, blogs, and quizzing and assessment features. This software can be one-stop shopping areas for students to access all the materials needed for a particular class. Examples of learning management systems include Moodle, Blackboard, Canvas, Schoology, Edmodo, Haiku Learning, My Big Campus, and a number of others.

Each of them has advantages and disadvantages. Our recommendation is that schools adopt one system as an institution, so that students get all of their digital content from one site.

Instead of using an LMS, some teachers have simply printed up a short notes sheet with a QR code on the top. Scanning the QR code with a smartphone app leads students to their video, and they take notes directly on the paper handout.

We have recently noticed a new breed of LMS that is built around the concept of game-based learning, or gamification. Instead of students going to a site to access content and interact with it, there is a gaming component where students can unlock conditionally released options and quests. Once students have completed a quest, they can earn experience points or badges. Teachers are using these points and badges as an alternate way to report progress because it connects with students in a familiar way.

I Want Specific Tools

Writing a book that recommends specific tech tools is difficult because technology changes so quickly. If you are in search of just the right tool for you, we have created and placed a series of videos on our website that features several tools for video creation, hosting, and all things technological for the flipped classroom. You can find these videos at http://FlippedClass.com/tools. You can also scan the following QR code to reach this website.

FIGURE 2.1 A quick response code that leads to http://FlippedClass.com/tools.

Finding the Time

Time is an elusive commodity. Where can you find the time to create all these videos, post them on a website, build in interactivity, and recreate your classroom activities? We wish we had a magical answer to tell you how to find the time, but we don't. To be honest, successful flipped class teachers just make the time, and even more successful flipped teachers collaborate and work together to maximize their time. Flipping your class will not make teaching easier, but it will make it better. We carved out time before or after school when we committed to making this happen. We were seeing such positive results that we felt we had to do this for our students, and that the extra work necessary to accomplish this task was worth it to us.

If your school or district leadership is supportive of the flipped classroom model, there are creative ways they can give you the time you will need to get started. The following are suggestions you and your school leadership might discuss:

- Hire substitute teachers for a day, and have two teachers plan and create videos and in-class activities.

- Use Professional Learning Team time to create shared video assets and other learning objects.

- Schedule common planning time for teachers.

- Use staff professional learning time to focus on flipping the class.

Training Yourself, Students, and Parents

The last hurdle to flipping a class is for all who are involved to get the appropriate training to implement the model well. There are two primary aspects of training to address.

Teach Students How to Watch Videos

A common mistake teachers make is assigning videos and assuming students will watch them. Students need to know *how* to watch an instructional video. We have discovered that this is not something that will come naturally to them. Students need specific instructions on how to *interact* with the videos. We suggest you watch the first few videos in class with your students while modeling how you want them to interact. Pause the video frequently and discuss how they should be listening, viewing, and thinking about the subject matter. Then have students individually watch the next video in class while you supervise and ensure they are appropriately learning from the video. Keep in mind that not every student will master all the content from any video after viewing it. The point of the video is to introduce content so that students can master the content *in class* with the real expert present—the teacher. We did this for an entire week with our high school chemistry students. We have heard from some middle school teachers that it has taken up to three weeks to teach their students how to interact with video content.

Get the Training You Need

Learning how to flip a math class is not just about assigning a video and working on problems and worksheets in class. It is so much more. You must plan, engage, develop, and revise. Find what works best for you in your setting and take what works. We like to say there is not one way to flip a class. Each flipped classroom looks different, and it should.

Some teachers have assigned a video as homework and discovered that students didn't watch it—and have given up on the flipped class. Setting up a successful flipped class requires thought and planning. The best way to set yourself up for success is to network with other teachers who flip their classes, attend a training session or conference on flipping your class, and ask many questions. Teachers need to consider many things before they jump into a flipped class model.

In the next chapter, we address key considerations for the flipped math classroom, such as planning lessons, keeping students engaged, and managing the chaos.

Chapter 3

planning
for the
flipped classroom

WE ALL LEARNED HOW to plan a lesson, a unit, or an entire school year in our college education courses. Many of these models for planning lessons are effective, but when the flipped classroom model is in place, many of these frameworks need to be re-addressed. Most planning structures (and the teacher evaluation instruments) imply, or even explicitly state, that there will be some sort of upfront presentation of information to a whole group of students. In a fully flipped classroom, the direct instruction is at the individual level or in small groups, so the planning of a flipped lesson will require a modification of the lesson's planning and delivery cycle. The easiest adaptation is to make a time-shift in the lesson. Shift the direct instruction out of the classroom space, and the independent practice back into the class space. Complex rearrangements of lesson elements are also certainly possible in a flipped class. A simple shift in time and space allows a teacher to implement the flipped model even if they are working in an environment that does not allow much flexibility in lesson planning. In the following sections, we will break this down by looking at how to organize a unit, a week, and a day.

Flipping a Unit

How does planning a unit change when you implement a flipped model? In many ways, it is not necessary to change how you plan a unit. Figure 3.1 is a planning guide of a unit on place value used by Delia Bush, a fifth grade math teacher in Michigan. In it, she has identified learning objectives, tied this to practice and hands-on activities, and created a video. We assume most math teachers already have a list of objectives similar to the ones in this chart. Most likely, these are already in place in most classes, with the exception of the creation of a video. Therefore, the only new thing a teacher needs to do is create a flipped video.

Learning Goal (LG)	Video	Watch-Summarize-Question	Required Homework Questions
LG 1: I can read and write decimals to the thousandths.	2.1	What place value do you think would come after the thousandths place? Explain why you think that.	Assignment 2-1, questions 2-22
LG 2: I can read and write numbers to the thousands.	2.2	How are the numbers "one hundred two thousand" and "one hundred and two thousandths" different?	Assignment 2-2, questions 1-5 and 14-21
LG 3: I can compare decimals to the thousandth.	2.3	Using the digits 1, 2, 3, and 4, what are the largest and smallest numbers you can make?	Assignment 2-3, questions 16-27
LG 4: I can add decimals and whole numbers with and without regrouping.	2.4	Explain why Tyler has the wrong sum for this addition sentence and explain how to find the correct sum. $35.2 + 1.46 = 4.98$	Assignment 2-4, questions 4-6 Assignment 2-5, questions 11-13
LG 5: I can subtract decimals and whole numbers with and without regrouping.	2.5	Write about a real-world situation in which you would need to add or subtract decimals.	Assignment 2-4, questions 7-9 Assignment 2-6, questions 4-6
LG 6: I can use different mathematical properties to compute mental math.	2.6	How can you use the Associative and Commutative Properties to help solve a problem mentally?	Assignment 2-7, questions 1-5 and 7-8
LG 7: I can round decimals to the nearest whole number, tenth, and hundredth.	2.7	Explain in words how you would round 10.239 to the nearest whole number.	Assignment 2-8, questions 1-9
LG 8: I can solve story problems involving adding and subtracting whole numbers and decimals.	2.8	You get to take a turn at writing story problems. Story problems have 3 sentences: a statement (about the 1st #), a statement (about the 2nd #), and a question that needs to be solved. Your job is to write a story problem (using at least 3 complete sentences) that goes with any of the learning goals from this unit.	Assignment 2-5, questions 14-15 Assignment 2-6, questions 7-10

FIGURE 3.1 Fifth grade math planning guide for a unit on place value.

One benefit of taking this approach is that it presses us as teachers to be very organized with content. The process of writing down objectives and creating or curating appropriate learning objects is a powerful process that teachers should implement regardless of whether they flip. Figure 3.1 is an example of such an organizing document. This kind of careful planning helps teachers to be thoughtful about which resources and assessments best fit each objective. This process is also helpful to those who often fly a bit by the seats of their pants—us included! Before we flipped our classes, we often walked in and "taught" what we wanted or just explained what was next in the curriculum. When we got serious about the flipped classroom, we realized we had to be much more organized about how we were teaching. This single exercise dramatically helped us to think through what was taught, how it was taught, and what things we should stop teaching.

Flipping a Week

Once a teacher plans a unit, how do they plan for a week? In many ways, a teacher's planning cycle does not need to change too dramatically. If a teacher has a flipped video they have created or curated, they need to build in a few extra steps to ensure that students don't just watch the video, but also interact with it. Here are a few suggestions for how to modify a typical weekly planning guide with the flip in mind:

- Give extra time and/or advance notice. Don't assign a video for one night and expect all students to complete the homework. Students may need more advance notice. Some students are overprogrammed and are on the go from the moment school ends. Trying to get some time in front of an internet-connected device at the last minute may be a challenge for such students.

- Allow some choice. Not every student needs to watch every video. The key is not that they *watched* something, but rather that they *learned* something. For example, if there is an online simulation that teaches the principles of plate tectonics, have students interact with that *instead* of watching a video.

Flipping a Day

Flipping a day in isolation (as a teaching strategy) can often be more difficult than flipping a whole unit or a class. This is because students are often not "trained" in learning in a flipped classroom setting. However, many teachers' first entry point in the flipped classroom is to flip a few lessons. They may only use a flipped lesson once every week or two. The key to flipping a day is to have the lower level cognitive content presented on video and have an engaging activity during class time.

Keeping Students Engaged

When Jon first started to flip his Earth and space science course, he wanted to have many hands-on activities for his students to engage with during the class time. At first, he had students doing experiments and activities almost every day. He soon realized that he was doing too many labs. The pace for his students was too frantic, and they got to the point where they were just trying to get through the labs instead of really learning from them. What his students needed was more time to simply work on assigned class problems and exercises. He realized students needed to practice and process their learning individually with his help.

We have also seen the other extreme where teachers have students watch a video at home and complete worksheets in class, but students aren't offered any hands-on activities. This repeats day after day. Though students need time to process and practice, they also need engaging activities with which to interact. If the only change you make is flipping the time of day you deliver direct instruction and have students complete worksheets, you have not made pedagogical changes; you have merely made temporal changes.

There are two ends of the spectrum where a teacher can err, and landing on either end of the spectrum can lead to disengaged students (see Figure 3.2). Try to find a balance, a "sweet spot," where students have time for engaging hands-on activities and time to process content with you, the expert teacher, present.

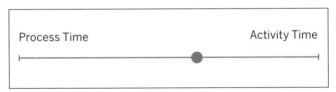

FIGURE 3.2 Finding the balance, or "sweet spot," between time for processing content and activity time maximizes student engagement.

Managing the Chaos

One of the biggest struggles flipped class teachers face is choosing which students to help and when. Because teachers are constantly moving around the room assisting students, what often happens is the students who are the most demanding get the most help and attention. As you know, the most demanding students are not always the ones who need the most help. In a flipped class, we need to be cognizant of which students need more help, which ones are ready for the next challenge, and which ones have learned something incorrectly and need clarification. There are no easy ways to determine which students need the most assistance. That changes from day to day and even moment to moment. Frankly, this is part of the art of teaching. The dance of the classroom is a difficult one, but it must be managed.

We had students come find us when they needed help, but this resulted in too many students standing in line and waiting. This also affected how willing students were to find us. One strategy you might try to identify students in need is to employ a visual cue. Cara Johnson, an anatomy teacher in Texas, uses a set of three colored plastic cups at each table to create a quick visual trigger identifying which students need help. A green cup indicates that students are fine and do not need any help; a yellow cup indicates that the group has a question but does not need an immediate answer; and a red cup indicates that the table of students are at an impasse and need immediate assistance. Using a system such as the cups helps students subtly indicate to their teacher their level of need, and it gives a teacher a way to assess individual and group needs quickly.

In the next chapter, we will explore some ways to enhance your flipped classroom with innovative and interactive resources.

Chapter 4

flipping with interactive math resources

FLIPPING A CLASS inherently provides a teacher with additional class time to involve students in more active learning. This may be a lab in a science class, a discussion of literature in an English class, or a public debate in a social studies class. What is the analogous activity in a math class? Fortunately, a large number of interactive activities are available for the math teacher. In addition to hands-on and participatory work, students can contribute to the collection of interactive material through the creation of their own content.

Math Manipulatives

Math teachers have been using manipulatives effectively for many years. Activities with manipulatives help students better understand and apply important math concepts by tactilely *manipulating* items that physically represent abstract mathematical concepts. A problem math teachers often face is a lack of time to use the power of manipulatives fully in class. Because the flipped classroom causes a drastic rethinking of how class time is used, teachers can take advantage of manipulatives more frequently. Missy Northingham, a sixth grade math teacher in San Antonio, Texas, flipped her class and uses the extra time with her students for a variety of activities, such as creating factor label cards that students use to convert units of measurement (Figure 4.1).

If virtual tools are more your speed, there is a library of virtual manipulatives at Utah State University that students can interact with online. Find the National Library of Virtual Manipulatives at http://nlvm.usu.edu/en/nav/vlibrary.html.

FIGURE 4.1 After making factor label cards, students in Missy Northingham's sixth grade math class take the cards home and watch their teacher demonstrate how to use them in a flipped video. This accelerates students' understanding of key concepts and it helps them ask specific questions the following day.

Interactive Simulations and Tools

There are many online simulations for students that can take the place of direct instruction. These simulations serve as simple inquiry activities, where students explore mathematical concepts on their own or delve deeper into a particular topic. These simulations typically engage students with graphs, geometric shapes, and other real-world applications of math concepts, allowing students to interact with virtual objects and learn from them. Students are able to explore key concepts simply by changing variables and discovering for themselves what would occur. These types of simulations are very useful and can take the place of direct instruction through flipped videos. Students can learn more deeply through discovery, rather than just interacting with videos on the same topic. Learning through these simulations can also be faster than some inquiry labs because of how efficiently students can manipulate variables in a virtual environment.

Following are some examples of online simulations and other software that may be helpful for the flipped math classroom:

- Geogebra (http://geogebra.org) is not just for geometry. There are activities for all levels of math. You can also view teacher-created lessons at http://geogebratube.org.

- Desmos (https://www.desmos.com) is an online graphing calculator that allows students to interact with mathematical concepts.

- PHET Interactive Simulations (http://phet. colorado.edu) is a free resource made by a team at the University of Colorado that provides math and science simulations you can manipulate.

- Explore Learning Gizmos (http://www.explorelearning.com) is a subscription service with math and science simulations.

- Many textbooks also include simulations that directly tie into the content teachers may already be teaching.

Manipulatives and simulations are ideal, though not necessary, for teachers who have access to an interactive whiteboard. Small groups of students can gather around the interactive board and collaboratively experience these simulations together. Many of these simulations also have guided activities that may be valuable in helping students make sense of the content.

Student-Created Content

Once students understand the content, it is valuable to have them demonstrate it through the creation of their own instructional or explanatory material. Crystal Kirch, a math teacher in southern California, has her students create their own videos as an assessment tool. She asserts this is important because "students need the opportunity to discuss math and speak in an academic way about the math. It becomes the teacher's job to give them the appropriate guidance necessary to be able to discuss math." To help students do this, she has them create a video for which they write their own word problems that are modeled after examples Crystal gives them. Students can collaborate by having a fellow student solve the problem, or evaluate the problem after it is solved. Students then work together to explain and record the concept using a simple whiteboarding app before posting it to a blog.

Another master of student-created content is Eric Marcos, a middle school math teacher in Santa Monica, California. Eric has successfully established an after-school math club, where students volunteer to develop and create math videos for their peers (November, 2012). Students use screencasting apps and take on fake names to preserve their anonymity.

Erin Richerson, an eighth grade math teacher in Olathe, Kansas, features students in her videos as guest hosts (Figure 4.2). The students take on roles as guest experts and help her explain to other students the concepts they have mastered in ways their peers can understand. She also brings students in to participate in her "Hotspot" videos, which assist students who are struggling with particular math concepts. In these videos, she and a student think through and discuss certain practice or review problems without working out the entire solution.

FIGURE 4.2 Students from Erin Richerson's eighth grade math class use a smartphone to video record an algebra tutorial.

Making math more interactive and participatory is one way to enhance your class time with students, but you can also use resources that are more traditional in a flipped class. The next chapter explores how the implementation of student choice and autonomy can enhance the use of traditional resources.

Chapter 5

traditional resources and choice in flipped learning

ONE OF THE MISCONCEPTIONS about the flipped class is that it is just learning through video. From the outside, it can appear that a flipped classroom is only about watching videos before class and then doing other things during class time. Though most teachers start with this, they quickly realize that the real benefit of flipping the classroom is reinventing the class time. What happens in class is far more important than video creation and consumption.

Information can clearly be transferred using methods other than video. Students can read textbooks or online content and learn through the inquiry process, learn by doing, and learn in numerous other ways. This chapter explores tools that complement instructional video and that can help teachers get away from lecture as the primary means of disseminating information. We also present the idea that giving students a choice can increase their engagement.

Some teachers have noted that they have been flipping their class for a long time—decades, in fact. They send students home to read a textbook and expect them to come to class prepared to engage in higher-order thinking. Pre-teaching models have been around for well over two centuries (Thayer Method, inverted classroom, etc.). So are these flipping methods? We encourage educators to avoid semantic arguments about whether something is flipped or not, and focus on whether the needs of students are being met. Pedagogically, there is little difference between assigning a text to read, an activity to complete, a PowerPoint to click through, or a video to view. All of these methods are designed around the expectation that students will come to class prepared. Flipping the class with video is simply a way to reach a video-saturated culture in a familiar medium.

Textbooks

Most schools still issue students textbooks at the beginning of the year. Though many of these textbooks are now digital, they are textbooks nonetheless. We are not against textbooks. We see them as a valuable resource to help students learn. Flipped videos should not take the place of reading as a rule. However, be strategic about any textbook readings you assign. Keep assigning readings where appropriate and use flipped videos where appropriate.

Other Readings

Clearly, textbooks should not be the only reading resource we provide for students to interact with. We want students to read other text relating to math. Students can also read about current events related to math. Because some of these articles may contain inaccessible vocabulary or concepts, students may need to read the more complex content in class. In this case, students would need an expert interpreter to help them access the content in these higher-level articles.

The Ideal Flipped Class: Choice

When we were traditional teachers, we simply taught our lessons to the whole group on our timetable. Students then went home and did homework. They got their information by attending class. Then we started flipping our classrooms, and students received their information through video. For many reasons, this was better than the previous system, but there was still only *one* way to get information.

As we moved into our third year of flipping our class, we realized that not all students learn best from any one method (lecture or video). As a result, we realized that teaching through multiple modalities is the best way to organize a flipped classroom. We began to give students choices on how they want to learn new content. Some chose to learn by reading the textbook, others liked learning through videos, and still others needed hands-on activities to learn. Instead of simply assigning one reading, or one video, or one online simulation, we suggest you offer students a variety of options.

One particular student approached Jon and asked if he could skip the flipped videos. He asked if he could just read the textbook instead. The answer was clearly, yes! If a student can learn better by reading a textbook, then there is no need for teachers to require them to view a video. If students learn better by reading, let them read; if they learn more effectively through online simulations, let them simulate. This may seem a bit disorganized and chaotic, but students naturally consume information in many different ways, and ultimately, giving students a choice will help them all be more engaged in the learning process.

One way to implement choice into your flipped class is to create a choice board (Figure 5.1). The boards are set up so students cannot simply complete the easy activities and avoid the hard ones. Instead, choice boards are set up so that students must do one knowledge-level activity, followed by an application-level activity, followed by an analysis-level activity. The choice board approach uses Bloom's taxonomy as a basis for determining levels of cognition.

Developing choice boards and the corresponding activities will take a considerable amount of time. We do not recommend that teachers who are new to the flipped class start with choice boards. Developing a library of videos and getting quality activities in class will need to be the first priority, but as a teacher moves along, choice boards could be a powerful addition to their class.

	Knowledge/ Understanding- Level Activities	Application- Level Activities	Higher Order/ Hands-On Activities
Activity 1	Read textbook and take notes	Worksheet (Odd questions)	Interactive Activity A
Activity 2	Watch video, take notes, and interact with the video using online tools	Worksheet (Even questions)	Interactive Activity B
Activity 3	Search the learning objective online and summarize your findings	Interactive Online Simulation. Meet with your teacher and explain the concepts	Student Project Design your own interactive activity that demonstrates the key point of this objective

FIGURE 5.1 This example choice board gives students the freedom to choose the activity that most appeals to them.

One of the most commonly asked questions about a flipped classroom is, "If I'm not lecturing anymore, what am I supposed to do during class?" In the next chapter, we offer some specific examples of how to reinvent your class time.

Chapter 6

rethinking class time

BECAUSE A FLIPPED classroom frees up more time with students, the most important question to answer is what to do with the recovered class time. Ultimately, there is no "right" answer to that question, but it is imperative that teachers begin the process of rethinking how to use the face-to-face time in class with students together as a group. This chapter focuses on some ways in which you can maximize class time to help students move to deeper levels of understanding and truly learn math.

What Should Math Teachers Do with Face-to-Face Class Time?

Books about math instruction in the digital age suggest that we should be teaching through inquiry, projects, and simulations. After talking with numerous math teachers who have flipped their classes, we've found that this is not always happening. In fact, many teachers we spoke with felt guilty because their students spend the majority of their class time working individually or in small groups solving math problems.

Having students solve problems in class is common practice and acceptable to most teachers because students *need* practice to master concepts; however, it is important that teachers incorporate inquiry, projects, and simulations as well.

Think of this as a continuum. On one side, a teacher uses class time for worksheets and practice. On the other side of the continuum, you have students engaging in higher-order cognitive activities that challenge and enrich. Flipped class teachers who use class time for practice alone are shortchanging their students. Yet teachers who teach through inquiry and projects alone don't often get through the required curriculum. You need a mix of both. Many math teachers want to assign higher-order tasks, but struggle to find the time to do so. Flipped learning recuperates class time so that more higher-order cognitive tasks can take place in the classroom, with the content area expert in the room to assist.

Individualized Instruction

We can summarize all of the strategies in this chapter with the term "individualized instruction." Under a more traditional model of instruction, students receive instruction according to the pre-established pace of the class. In a flipped classroom, students get assistance with content right when they need it.

Guided and Independent Practice

In a flipped class, students have more time for guided practice. Math teachers have traditionally sent students home to work on assigned problems. These problems are, in general, more cognitively complex than many students are ready to handle on their own. As a result, many students struggle to complete these tasks independently. For whatever reason, they missed crucial content in class and simply couldn't do the homework. Students then came to class frustrated with incomplete work and deeply rooted misconceptions. Simply flipping your class gives students time to work on problems with the teacher present. This is revolutionary for learning because teachers can spend considerably more time circulating around the classroom assisting students. This individualized instructional assistance time may be the single greatest benefit to a flipped classroom. Students who struggle get the help they need. With the increased student-teacher time, there is simply more time to assist struggling students—and there is also more time to challenge the high-achieving students who are ready for more.

Students make many common mistakes when working on math problems. For example, when students add fractions of unlike denominators, many fail to find the lowest common denominator first. When multiplying numbers with exponents, students often multiply the exponents rather than add the exponents. Students without immediate correction repeat common mistakes like these at home, and this reinforces incorrect math. If students make these mistakes during class time, teachers can quickly correct them and reinforce proper math processes through supervised practice.

Small-Group Tutorials

During guided and independent practice, teachers often have several students who struggle with similar content. Recovered class time allows teachers to engage them in small groups to review difficult concepts or clear up jointly held misconceptions.

Students may struggle with problems that involve the order of operations or how to determine the vertex of a parabola. Teachers may bring those students together for a mini tutorial at the whiteboard and direct them as they solve problems, while students who do not need assistance work independently. Teachers can also take students to a digital whiteboard and record the mini help sessions. The students in the small group now have access to a video recording of the discussion to review later. In our experience, students found this level of personalization very helpful because they had a tutorial made just for them, which covered the difficult concepts with which *they* were struggling. These help sessions also became available to other students to access in case they needed assistance with the same topic. Having a peer group working together on a topic they all struggle with helps students to collectively understand and apply the math. The use of small-group tutorials also allows for a more efficient use of teachers' time by allowing them to help multiple students struggling with similar content.

Challenge Problems

Stacey Roshan, a high school math teacher in Maryland, uses the recovered class time gained from flipped learning to differentiate instruction for her high-performing students. She has students who quickly master basic concepts begin working to solve what she calls challenge problems. Stacey's challenge problems are those that she believes her elite students could not solve if she were to assign them as homework. Because some of her students' class time is now available to work on challenge problems, they tackle the problems in small groups and find great satisfaction as they push beyond the curriculum and take learning deeper.

Peer Tutoring

Although there is value in students wrestling with content on their own, it is amazing to observe students helping each other learn. Students who have just learned something can often be better teachers than we are because the learning process is so fresh in their minds. A novice who has just learned something new can provide meaningful insight to his or her peers about learning the same concept. This creates a collaborative atmosphere where students work together to comprehend a new concept. It also builds a sense of community. In many ways, this mirrors the ad hoc study groups many of us organized in college, but it now happens in K–12 classrooms, with the added benefit that the teacher is present to help the group when it reaches an impasse.

Going Over Homework

Before flipping her classroom, Erin Richerson, an eighth grade math teacher we mentioned earlier, spent a considerable amount of class time reviewing and grading homework from the previous night. She did this because it gave students a chance to clarify any misconceptions, and it gave them the opportunity to see math problems solved correctly. She would often have her students grade each other's assignments, which helped students receive instant feedback and provided her with much-needed preparation time.

After implementing the flipped class model, her class time shifted. Instead of spending the beginning of class reviewing work from the previous night, she reviews the day's work at the end of a class. This takes much less time, because she spends the majority of class time working with students individually to clarify misconceptions and correct mistakes.

Peer Instruction

Teachers all over the globe use the peer instruction teaching method to engage students during class time. Dr. Eric Mazur, a physics professor at Harvard University, developed peer instruction in 1991. He was dissatisfied with students' conceptual learning in his traditional lecture classes, so he looked for a way to reinvigorate his class and help students develop deeper understandings of key physics content. Peer instruction, which is often paired with just-in-time teaching for out-of-class work, is backed by 20 years of research that demonstrates increased learning outcomes, including problem-solving skills, conceptual understanding, and decreasing the gender gap in the sciences (Schell, Lukoff, & Mazur, 2013). Studies conducted by math teacher Troy Faulkner in the high school mathematics context at Byron High School in Byron, Minnesota, also demonstrate that when peer instruction is used in conjunction with flipped learning, student achievement is increased (Fulton, 2012).

Peer instruction has seven nonnegotiable steps. We adapted the following from Julie Schell's blog post at http://blog.peerinstruction.net/2012/07/03/ choreography-of-a-flipped-classroom.

1. Assign a "coverage" task — a reading, video, or activity — or provide a mini lecture on a particular concept. These are videos that students would typically watch before class in a flipped classroom. Example: Before class, Troy had his students watch this video on radicals as rational exponents: bit.ly/peerflipmath.

2. Begin a round of questioning (Round 1): Pose a question related to the coverage activity to students and solicit individual responses. Students must commit to one answer. You can collect responses with low-tech tools such as cards, or higher-tech tools such as a student response system. Troy had his students respond to the question in Figure 6.1.

I can write radicals as rational exponents and vice versa plus simplify expressions

Evaluate without a calculator $(-32)^{-3/5}$

Simplify

$$\sqrt[3]{5} \cdot \sqrt{5^3} \qquad \frac{2c^{1/8}}{c^{-1/16} \cdot c^{1/8}} \qquad \frac{ab}{\sqrt[3]{c}} \qquad \left(a^{-2/3}\right)^{-1/6}$$

FIGURE 6.1 A sample question for students following a coverage task.

The video does not directly answer this example question. It is an application of the concepts found in the video. The key in developing good peer instruction questions is to allow students to apply conceptual understanding. These are typically at higher-order levels of cognition (think Applying or above on Bloom's taxonomy).

3. Analyze student responses.

4. Group students based on response.

5. Put students into groups of between two and four students in which not all of the students have chosen the same answer. Cue them to find someone with a different answer and try to defend their answers with reasoning. During

this conversation, students try to understand the question together. To see the students discussing the question in Figure 6.1 during their peer instruction, visit bit.ly/peermathflip2.

6. Begin Round 2 of questioning. Re-poll the students. You should expect to see a shift to the right answer after discussion.

7. Discuss any misconceptions. Not all students will get the answer correct, so a class discussion about the question at hand is worth the conversation.

If you would like to read more about this method, we recommend Mazur's book *Peer Instruction: A User's Manual* (Mazur, 1997). He spends the first six chapters discussing the model and then the rest of the book describing specific physics activities you can do with your students.

Troy, an early adopter of peer instruction for high school math, has several tips for effectively using peer instruction:

- **How often should you use peer instruction?** Troy uses about 20% of his class time for peer instructional sessions, because he still sees the need for students to work individually on number sense and math cognition.

- **Which part of class is best suited for peer instruction?** Though Troy typically uses peer instruction at the beginning of the class, he has found it useful to break up longer-blocked classes with multiple peer instructional sessions.

- **How difficult should questions be for peer instruction?** Troy has found it is ideal to use questions that 30% to 70% of the students will answer correctly. There is no need to use this method if the question is too easy. If it is too hard, the activity only reinforces students' misconceptions and misunderstandings.

- **What types of questions are best suited for peer instruction?** Troy has found that multiple-choice questions are highly effective in his introductory classes. His advanced math students do better with more open-ended questions.

There are a number of polling tools that can help facilitate peer instruction in your flipped classroom. This category of tools allows teachers to facilitate discussion around a question or prompt related to a video students viewed before class. To see a list of the tools that do this, go to http://flippedclass.com/tools.

Structured Discussions

Crystal Kirch uses some of her class time for what she calls structured discussions. Her lesson on quadratic models is one example of how she leads this type of discussion. Before class, students watch a short video on how to use the quadratic equation. In class, students divide into groups and apply quadratic models to the punting of a football. They use their understanding of quadratic functions to respond to a variety of prompts that ultimately leads them to understand why the quadratic equation best models a punted football, rather than a cubic equation. Here are a couple questions Crystal asks:

- What is the farthest the football will travel?

- Does the "a" in the quadratic always need to be a number with the absolute value less than 1 to correctly model the behavior of a punted football?

The brilliance of Crystal's structured discussions is that her students use class time to develop deeper understandings. They're not just learning how to solve the quadratic formula; they are learning how to apply quadratic functions in the real world.

Now that you have flipped your class, you can take it even further by using the flipped-mastery approach. The next chapter explains how a flipped math class can transition to an asynchronous mastery learning environment where students must demonstrate mastery of objectives before moving on.

Chapter 7

mastery learning
in the
flipped classroom

ALTHOUGH WE ADDRESSED in detail the approach we call flipped-mastery in our first book, we thought we would dig a bit deeper into the topic as it pertains to math education. Mastery learning is not a new development in education; it was developed in the middle of the twentieth century by Benjamin Bloom of Bloom's taxonomy fame. Essentially, mastery learning is a system in which learners must demonstrate understanding, or "mastery," of a particular topic before moving through the rest of the course material. Mastery learning works especially well for subjects that are linear in sequence and build off material learned earlier in the course. Learn A before learning B before learning C, because you will not understand C without understanding B, and you will not understand B without understanding A. Mathematically based sciences, math, grammar, and mechanics of language are subjects that lend themselves nicely to this approach.

In a flipped-mastery setting, students work through the course material at their own pace by accessing instructional video content, problem sets, activities, demonstrations, and other learning objects when they are ready for them. Operating in an asynchronous environment like this allows students the flexibility to learn at a pace that is appropriate for them. It has an added advantage in that it can solve issues of access for students without sufficient technology at home. In a flipped-mastery classroom, video content can easily be accessed in class. Flipped-mastery is often the second iteration of a flipped classroom that builds off the video library a teacher has developed through the first phase of flipping his or her class.

Flipped-mastery places more control of learning into the hands of the students because it allows them the flexibility to create their own schedules of learning based around their own learning needs and styles. Some students may need some additional support and structure in a mastery environment, and providing them with daily, weekly, or monthly goals is one way to help students avoid getting behind. This system also allows high-achieving students to move more quickly through the course material and gives them time to work on independent projects of their own design.

Flipped-Mastery Examples

Next, let's look at two successful implementations of the flipped-mastery model.

Graham Johnson

Graham Johnson is a Grade 10 math teacher at Okanagan Mission Secondary School in Kelowna, British Columbia, Canada. Graham teaches at a high-achieving school and felt that his teaching practice was going fairly well. He was doing a great job teaching; however, he was continually frustrated that his kids were not learning. His lectures were moderately engaging, but his students' exam scores varied widely.

Graham's school was fortunate enough to have access to many resources. It is in a community that values high student performance and active involvement by students in all that the school and community has to offer. This resulted in many students missing class because they were taking full advantage of these opportunities. Graham's absent students would dutifully acquire the lecture notes from their peers, but that was never an adequate way for his students to learn the missed material. Graham was reaching a point of frustration. Then he heard from a colleague about the concept of making videos for students rather than lecturing new content. He decided to try it. Realizing he needed some training in this concept, Graham attended the 2010 Flipped Learning Conference (FlipCon 2010). Graham got excited about the concept of flipped-mastery after attending a session by Colorado math teacher Phil McIntosh. By leveraging the power of asynchronous instruction and assessment, Graham knew he could use existing technologies to free up his time and personally meet the individual learning needs of his students. In doing so, Graham learned how flipped-mastery helps teachers turn over control of the learning process to students. Graham flipped his class in 2010, jumped directly into the flipped-mastery model, and never looked back.

In Canada, a score of 50% is a passing grade, but Graham never felt that was an adequate measure of content mastery. Graham successfully raised the bar in his class by implementing flipped-mastery. Before using the flipped-mastery model, some students would fail an exam, yet the class would march on because new content had to be covered. Now, as students progress through content, they receive immediate and appropriate feedback precisely when they need it, and students are not forced to move forward until they are ready to do so. The feedback loop continues until the students have demonstrated their learning. In the past, Graham hoped for success. Now, through flipped-mastery, success is inevitable.

Graham uses a pre-test "hot seat," where he asks a student a few key questions to ascertain whether that student is ready to take an exam. Graham states, "It is child abuse to put a test in front of a kid when I knew they were going to fail, and they knew they were going to fail. They would stare at the wall and sometimes cry, knowing they would fail. This was not getting us anywhere." The hot seat interview prevented unnecessary stress and eliminated inevitable failure by screening unprepared students out and providing them with necessary remediation to ensure future success. Sometimes his students knew little about a subject, but inevitably, all students began to learn more. Now they *earn* the opportunity to take a test rather than having one thrust in front of them. Sometimes students who are not ready are grateful for the opportunity to better prepare themselves before taking an exam. Even those ready to pass may not be ready to proceed. This is an opportunity to be proactive rather than reactive.

One aspect of the flipped-mastery class Graham appreciates is the ability to engage students with interactive activities every day. He typically begins with question-and-answer time, follows with a review, and then moves on to an activity. For some students in his self-paced class, the activity is a preview of content they will learn in the future; for others, it is exactly what they need at the time. Some are beyond this point in their learning and use the activity as a review. By implementing flipped-mastery, Graham can explore the effectiveness of other technologies and techniques, such as interactive whiteboards, active learning, and learning journals, which can all help support the metacognitive component of deep learning. "I care about the end of learning," says Graham, when asked why he finds flipped learning so useful. "I don't care about the mess along the way."

The greatest benefit of the flipped-mastery model is the strong relationships it fosters between teachers and students. Initially, Graham feared that the model would give him less time to get to know his students, but he found that his student-teacher relationships have become better than ever. As with many flipped-mastery teachers, Graham is now making better connections with students because it is easier to recognize, diagnose, and help them overcome the learning challenges they face. In addition, flipped-mastery students often talk to Graham about aspects of their lives that are unrelated to school, giving Graham the chance to encourage students to pursue their dreams.

The Algebros

Aaron met Tim Kelly in 2009 on a bus in Washington, DC, heading toward the U.S. Capitol as part of the Presidential Award for Excellence in Math and Science Teaching event. Tim is a math teacher at Baumholder High School, a Department of Defense Education Activity (DODEA) school in Germany. Tim and Aaron were both recipients of the award that year and serendipitously sat next to each other on the bus that day. During that short trip, Aaron told Tim about his flipped classroom work. Tim returned to Germany and told his colleagues, Michael Brust, Corey Sullivan, and Spencer Bean (the rest of the Algebros team—yes, they call themselves the Algebros), about flipped-mastery.

The Algebros jumped directly into flipped-mastery. Corey, a math teacher at Kaiserslautern High School, had used elements of traditional mastery for a long time, so using video to help facilitate his mastery class was a natural transition for him. The Algebros now split the workload when developing their flipped-mastery classrooms, producing content as a team while maintaining autonomy over how each chooses to manage his own classroom. They divide chapters, collaborate while developing material, and use vertical teaming and alignment to maintain continuity of content.

Given the transient nature of military personnel, a Department of Defense school can receive new students at any time, making every classroom a heterogeneous mix of ability levels. In reality, every classroom in every school around the world is heterogeneous, and flipped-mastery can help manage this reality. DODEA schools, however, amplify this effect, which creates a particularly difficult challenge. The Algebros use flipped-mastery to meet this challenge because it helps them attend to the individual needs of each new student. They assess new students and place them on to the math continuum, depending on their existing knowledge and skills. Because the Algebros all work together to vertically align their curricula, they can flexibly and fluidly move students between courses and teachers as needed. In fact, the Algebros have become so fluid that every level of math is covered in all of their classrooms. What this means is that students completing Algebra 1 can be found in classrooms with Algebra 2, Geometry, and Trigonometry students, rather than Algebra 1 students alone.

What the Algebros have discovered is that they can identify students' math deficiencies and help them overcome them better than ever because classes are so individualized. These teachers are flipped-mastery gurus who have created such a rich and individualized learning environment in which each student essentially has an Individual Education Plan (IEP). This is not the scary, paperwork-heavy, report-laden, "yet another meeting" type of IEP. Each student has his or her individual learning needs met daily. The Algebros have observed that their students are no longer working for the check mark or the score, but are working toward learning. Students are busy, bell to bell, with each student doing what he or she needs individually and thriving in the organized chaos of the flipped-mastery classroom. The teachers are busy interacting with students, diagnosing problems, conducting formative assessment, and helping all students learn. "We are so atypical," says Tim. "The bell rings, we all do a warm-up, we grade the warm-up, and then we touch base with every kid at least once. Every time a kid raises his hand, he gets what he needs. We run around class showing kids how to learn and we motivate kids. We are all coaches coming up with a plan for each kid individually."

The following is some advice the Algebros have for others who are interested in exploring flipped-mastery:

- *Planning* is the most important thing. Think through the logistics and prepare.

- Flipped-mastery can be frustrating, but *stick it out.* It is a great feeling when you feel the accountability shift from teacher to learner.

- This can be a lot of work, so *power through*, because student learning is worth it.

- *Work as a team,* or at least to have someone serve as a sounding board.

- Just *dive in,* go for it, and help a kid learn!

The Algebros are at three different schools now, but each is using the same material, providing each other with plenty of feedback to ensure continual improvement. Clearly, these guys work well together and are willing to put in the time to produce content and develop their courses, which is one reason for their success. They distribute all their resources at http://flippedmath.com.

Making the Jump to Flipped-Mastery

Jumping into flipped-mastery is a big step. Many teachers flip their class and never move to flipped-mastery. We say emphatically that the move we made from Flipped Class 101 to flipped-mastery was the best thing we ever did in our careers. It was hard, but the level of learning and the degree to which our students took ownership of their learning was proof to us that it was the right decision.

To learn more about how to implement the flipped-mastery model, we encourage you to read the second half of our first book, *Flip Your Classroom,* and read *Flipped Learning,* which has some teacher discussions about how they moved to flipped-mastery.

Some math teachers have gravitated toward the flipped-mastery approach, but others are trying to find a way to merge flipped learning with an inquiry-based approach to learning. The next chapter explains how inquiry and flipping can complement each other.

Chapter 8

inquiry
and
flipped learning

MANY MATH TEACHERS have taken the flipped learning model and adapted it to operate in conjunction with or alongside various other math teaching and learning strategies, including guided inquiry and investigative learning. Some have suggested that flipped learning is incompatible with more constructivist approaches to learning. However, given that flipped learning is a flexible and adaptable model, we feel these claims are unwarranted.

Guided Inquiry

Adam Johnson, whom we met at the beginning of the book, has structured his class in a way that teaches students to construct knowledge and skills on their own. He uses three levels of engagement for his students to guide them through the inquiry process:

- **Stage 1:** Students learn how to perform a task

- **Stage 2:** Students execute the task and collect data

- **Stage 3:** Students analyze data and construct a formula or function that explains their data

To understand how this concept can be applied in an eighth grade flipped math class, let's examine a lesson Adam uses to teach dilation and scaling of geometric shapes.

Stage 1. Students learn the process of scaling a shape through a flipped video prior to class. In this video, Adam demonstrates how to use graph paper to draw a given shape larger or smaller, while maintaining the aspect ratio. Students follow along and take appropriate notes. Adam does not present a comprehensive lesson about all aspects of dilation and scaling, but gives the students only the information they need to be able to appropriately engage the inquiry activity in class.

Stage 2. When students come to class, they find 20 shapes around the room, which they are asked to scale up or down on their own graph paper. To accomplish this task successfully, students need to have learned from Adam's video how to draw shapes on a coordinate grid and know how to dilate shapes larger and smaller.

Stage 3. At this stage, Adam's students analyze their shapes and the corresponding data of the shapes' diameter, perimeter, area, and other geometric measurements. From this data, students must deduce patterns and develop their own formula or function that explains the relationship between the changed variable (length of a side or diameter) and the resulting variable (perimeter or area). Students are expected to know not only *how* to dilate (which they learned from a video), but which rules govern shape dilations (which they determined on their own).

Adam could have easily explained in a video all there is to know about dilation, including any appropriate formulas, but doing so would have robbed his students of the rich learning opportunity afforded them through the inquiry process. This example of using video as a pre-training tool shows the power of merging flipped learning with inquiry learning without robbing either model of its inherent value.

Video Story Problems

Ben Rimes is a K–12 instructional technology coordinator for Mattawan Schools, in Mattawan, Michigan, who formerly taught K–6 technology courses for 7 years. Although he would not classify himself as a flipped learning practitioner, Ben has been leveraging the power of teacher- and student-created video as a teaching tool for many years through the use of what he calls "Video Story Problems." Ben's video story problem project features him or his students presenting a question through a video. These questions are often open-ended and are designed to generate discussion, rather than leading to a specific answer.

One particular video shows Ben and his 2-year-old daughter in a shopping mall. In this mall is a large piece of marble, roughly 6 feet in diameter, with water being pumped underneath it. His daughter can easily spin the marble, even though it weighs nearly 3 tons. After filming his daughter for a few seconds, he turns the camera back on himself and asks, "How is my 2-year-old daughter able to spin a 3-ton marble?" That is all he asks. He doesn't explain any of the phenomena that allow her to do so, but rather leaves the question in the hands of his students to think about, speculate, and research. In this situation, video is used as a tool to inspire students, generate interest, and provide a framework from which an in-class lesson can build. Ben's Video Story Problem page can be found at http://vimeo.com/channels/videostoryproblems.

Another great resource for videos designed to inspire and generate interest are from TED-Ed (http://ed.ted.com). TED-Ed collaborated with classroom teachers and professional animators to create animated video lessons that do not necessarily present a comprehensive explanation about a particular topic, but generate interest around a concept. The TED-Ed site not only is a repository of interesting videos, but also has tools available to build in interactivity with videos through embedded questions and writing prompts.

Ben uses video because it allows him to connect the real world to mathematics. He believes, "There is no substitution for real world situations, so Video Story Problems allow the teacher to actually bring a problem or example into the classroom." These scenarios help answer the "When am I ever going to use this?" question that students frequently ask of math teachers.

Students Creating Video Story Problems

Applying Ben's model for video, math teachers can get kids creating videos and making homework fun. Have them digitally capture the real world and bring it back to class. Don't worry about how to fit it into the curriculum, but put it into the hands of the students and see where it leads them. Another option is to use Mathematics Challenges (www.collaborativemathematics.org), a website that asks students to use video to show their solutions to math problems. This is a great way to give students some extra time to work out a solution, and it gives those who might be uncomfortable in front of the class a place to present. Start small, start simple, and find a way for the students to do all the work. Creation is the highest cognitive level of Bloom's taxonomy. Any opportunity you can find to have students create content will help them understand any topic more deeply.

Transitioning to project-based learning (PBL) is natural in a flipped classroom. The next chapter explains how flipped videos can support PBL.

Chapter 9

projects and project-based learning

THERE ARE MULTIPLE approaches to implementing projects in a math class. We are going to highlight two of these approaches: projects as summative assessment and project-based learning.

Projects as Summative Assessment

Brian Gervase, a math teacher in Mountain House, California, was an early adopter of the flipped class concept. In 2009, he came to one of our first conferences, returning home inspired to implement Flipped Class 101 in his classroom. After 2 years of using Flipped Class 101, Brian decided to implement flipped-mastery. Brian came to FlipCon 2014 and told us how he had initially overlooked the importance of moving beyond Flipped Class 101 to flipped-mastery, but was glad that he made the transition.

As with many flipped class practitioners, Brian did not stop there. He realized that he needed a second iteration of his flipped classroom to meet the needs of all of his students. Brian was recently asked to lead the opening of a new high school and was tasked with building flipped learning into the "DNA" of the math department. Brian took the challenge, and he is not only using flipped-mastery, but also implementing PBL. According to Brian, "A math teacher can no longer just teach process and algorithms. We now need our students to be able to create a product."

To that end, Brian and his team are developing creative projects that accompany each unit of study. In each unit, students are required to demonstrate mastery with two different forms of assessment:

- **The traditional math exam.** This is still paper-pencil, solve the problems, et cetera.

- **A project.** Students apply their learning on a specific topic, accessing higher-order thinking, moving away from just algorithmic math.

The Birthday Polynomial Project (http://FlippedClass.com/birthdaypolynomials) is one example of a unit Brian uses in his pre-calculus class. In this project, students use the digits of their birthday in a polynomial to create rational expressions, determine asymptotes, and find maximums and minimums. Brian expects them to explain the math behind their unique, un-copyable, "non-Google-able" problem.

PBL in the Math Classroom

Many teachers think they are doing PBL simply because they have their students do projects. In reality, however, PBL is much more than projects. According to the Buck

Institute for Education, PBL is a teaching method where students gain knowledge and skills by working for an extended period to investigate and respond to a complex question, problem, or challenge (definition taken from http://bie.org/about/what_pbl).

The Buck Institute has been studying the efficacy of PBL for many years. They have shown PBL to be an effective way to teach standards and content without the use of direct instruction. Many teachers using flipped learning have found that the extra time they gain allows them the flexibility to explore strategies like PBL while still maintaining a library of content that is delivered regularly or as needed. Science teachers in particular are excited about PBL because so many science, technology, engineering, and mathematics (STEM) projects are available for students.

Math is a natural fit for PBL, and flipped learning is proving to be a gateway for math teachers to give it a try. Even if a teacher does not teach a content-heavy subject that requires a lot of content delivery, flipped videos can be used in project-oriented courses such as robotics or engineering to teach background information or essential skills. Rather than teaching an entire class how to perform a particular task, make a tutorial that students can access when they are ready to learn. Because students come to class with such a wide variety of skills and backgrounds, making use of video as an asynchronous teaching tool is one way to meet the individual learning needs of students.

Robotics and engineering teacher Erin Hopkins runs an entirely project-based class. Her students prepare for competitions by designing, testing, and modifying robots. However, she has found that some of her students learn at different paces, especially when using drafting software. Some of her students are familiar with the software when they arrive, and others have no experience with it. Some of her students pick up the skills quickly; others need more time. To accommodate everyone, Erin uses instructional videos to teach the software rather than teaching the class as a whole. This allows the students to move through the content at their own pace, and it allows them to work on drafting projects that are in alignment with their current skill level. Given that all students view content while in class, some may hesitate to call this flipped learning. However, the term "in-flip" is often used to describe this use of asynchronous instruction in which all the work is done in class. The power of flipped learning goes beyond using video as homework. The power lies in the delivery of instruction to individual learners.

Chapter 10

conclusion

SOME EDUCATORS have asked us to provide a step-by-step guide to flipping their classrooms. Although this book serves to provide specific guidelines to math teachers, these should be just that—guidelines. There is no one way to flip your class. Nor should there be. The flipped class needs to be customized and contextualized for each teacher's class, for their school population, and for each teacher's personal style. The worst mistake you could make is to try to replicate everything in this book to flip your class. Instead, we want you to use this as a guide from which you will adopt practices that make the most sense in your context.

We had one goal in writing this—to move teachers away from the front of the room and to encourage teachers to create active learning environments where *all students* are engaged in their own learning. A recent whitepaper entitled *Teaching for Rigor: A Call for a Critical Instructional Shift* from the Marzano Research Labs discussed what instructional strategies educators are actually using in classrooms. Marzano (Marzano & Toth, 2014) and his group, which collected more than 2 million data points from the United States, found that:

- 58% of all classroom time is being used for interacting with new content. The majority of this time is dedicated to direct instruction.

- 36% of classroom time is used for practicing and deepening content.

- 6% of classroom time is used for cognitively complex tasks involving generating and testing hypotheses.

These numbers need to change, especially in the classrooms of math teachers. The teaching of math should not be just knowing how to compute and count. Students need to know how to apply math to the real world in a wide variety of situations and circumstances.

In case you feel we are unrealistic about the real world in which there are state tests, end-of-course exams, and high expectations, know that we are not—and we still believe there is a place for direct instruction and content delivery. Students often don't know what they don't know, and teachers can help them through that discernment process. We have much to teach our students, but the reality is that many of us desire to do more inquiry, more application, more differentiation, and more projects. Yet the tyranny of curriculum and the comfort of our old ways often keep us in a rut. We are seeing around the world that the flipped class is proving to be a way for math teachers to move toward more active forms of learning.

Take, for example, Crystal Kirch, whom you met several times in this book. Crystal was stuck in the cycle of direct instruction, worksheets, and assessment, with an occasional project thrown in for good measure. She first flipped her class using the Flipped Class 101 model, but soon realized she could do more. Her next step was to help her students to better interact with the video content. She developed what she calls the Watch-Summarize-Question (WSQ) technique (Bergmann & Sams, 2014) and saw an increase in student engagement and understanding. Her next step was to have students as creators of content. Crystal's students wrote their own math problems, and then made videos explaining how to solve those problems. Again, she saw her students deepen their understanding, with math videos explaining the problems. Her next step was to have her students get involved in project-based learning, and she soon hopes to extend the scope to include collaborative projects with students from around the world.

Crystal has customized and contextualized the flipped learning model for *her* situation, *her* style of teaching, and *her* students. In that spirit we encourage you to use this book as a guide. Do not consider it a set of rules that you must follow. Our challenge to you is to do what Crystal has done. Find the parts of the flipped classroom model that work for you and merge it with the good teaching practices you have been doing for years, or wish you could be doing.

We encourage you to take these action steps to get started:

- **Take an honest look.** What percentage of your class time is involved in direct instruction or practice? Before we flipped our classes, our numbers were similar to the data from the Marzano Research Labs, and you may be in a similar situation. Think carefully about how flipping your class could help your students spend less time with new content and more time working on more challenging cognitive tasks.

- **Choose to begin.** Flip at least one lesson, or start by recording your live lessons for 1 year. What one lesson or topic do students in your class typically struggle with, so that you find yourself repeating it over and over? That is the perfect lesson to be your first flip.

- **Communicate.** The flipped classroom may be a new concept for students, parents, and administrators. Before you flip, develop an action plan to share reasons why you are flipping your class and to communicate your expectations to all stakeholders, including students, parents, and administrators.

- **Plan your flip.** It can be difficult to jump right into a fully flipped class. It may be better for you to look carefully at your existing course materials and spend some time planning how each lesson might (or might not) be adapted to accommodate video as an instructional tool.

- **Learn more.** This book is an introduction for math teachers. Pick up a copy of *Flip Your Classroom* and the accompanying workbook. If you are at

all intrigued with the flipped-mastery model, the
second half of *Flip Your Classroom* focuses on how
to implement it.

The world of information has dramatically changed
since most of us were in school. We grew up in an
information-scarce world where information "lived" in
libraries, books, and the heads of our teachers. Today
we live in a saturated world where information is easily
accessible to anyone with an internet-ready device.
Whatever we teach, whether it is middle school life
science, Earth science, chemistry, biology, or AP Physics,
there is now an instructional video on YouTube that
teaches everything in the curriculum. There are count-
less videos on Newton's first law, on how to balance an
oxidation-reduction reaction, on the causes of earth-
quakes, on mitosis, and so on.

If a YouTube video can replace us, we should be replaced!
We realize this is a strong statement, but hear us out.
Teachers are no longer the keepers of information, so
our roles must change. We need to move away from
being disseminators of content and instead become
facilitators of learning. As we embrace our new roles,
we will be adding more value to our students' learning
experiences. Instead of being replaced by a computer or
a video, we are becoming more necessary and integral

to education—because only teachers can help students explore topics more deeply, and only a content-area and learning expert can diagnose where students struggle. In a flipped classroom, the teacher is actually more necessary, more needed, and more integral to the learning experience of all students. We are adding value beyond the content. We are ushering our students into an environment in which they take ownership of their learning.

Will you embrace the flipped classroom? Will you take on the challenge of changing your practice?

references

Bergmann, J., & Sams, A. (2012). *Flip your classroom: Reach every student in every class every day.* Eugene, OR: ISTE/ASCD.

Bergmann, J., & Sams, A. (2014). *Flipped learning: Gateway to student engagement.* Eugene, OR: ISTE.

Bloom, B. S. (1968). Learning for mastery. *UCLA-CSEIP Evaluation Comment, 2*, 1–12.

Fulton, K. (2012, June/July). Upside down and inside out: Flip your classroom to improve student learning. *Learning & Leading with Technology, 39*(8), 12–17.

Marzano, R., & Toth, M. (2014, March). *Teaching for rigor: A call for a critical instructional shift.* Rep. Marzano Research Labs. Retrieved from http://www.marzanocenter.com/essentials/teaching-for-rigor-landing.

Mazur, E. (1997). *Peer instruction: A user's manual.* Upper Saddle River, NJ: Prentice Hall.

November, A. C. (2012). *Who owns the learning?: Preparing students for success in the digital age.* Bloomington, IN: Solution Tree Press.

Schell, J., Lukoff, B., & Mazur, E. (2013). Catalyzing learner engagement using cutting-edge classroom response systems in higher education. In C. Wankel & P. Blessinger (Eds.), *Increasing student engagement and retention using classroom technologies: Classroom response systems and mediated discourse technologies* (pp. 233–261). Bingley, England: Emerald Publishing Group.